🔵 **Ready to uncover LeBron James' secrets?** 🔵

Dive into this exciting illustrated biography packed with fun facts, exclusive stories, and inspiring moments from LeBron's incredible life! Learn how a kid from Akron, Ohio, with big dreams and unstoppable determination became one of the greatest basketball players of all time.

🌟 Full of never-before-heard details about his passion for basketball, love for competition, and journey to the top, this book is perfect for fans aged 8 to 12 who want to know everything about LeBron! Get inspired by his story and let LeBron's legendary rise to NBA stardom fuel your own dreams of greatness! 💪✨

Copyright © 2024 All rights reserved.

No part of this publication may be reproduced, distributed, or transmitted in any form or by any means, including photocopying, recording, or other electronic or mechanical methods, without prior written permission from the publisher, except in the case of brief quotations embodied in critical reviews and certain other noncommercial uses permitted by copyright law.

Published by VendittoEditore.com

LeBron James was born on December 30, 1984, in Akron, Ohio. Growing up in a tough neighborhood, he was raised by his mother, Gloria James, who worked tirelessly to support him. Gloria's dedication and love helped shape LeBron into the determined and hardworking person he is today.

From a young age, LeBron showed a natural talent for sports. When he was just three years old, his mother gave him a basketball, and he quickly fell in love with the game. He spent countless hours dribbling and shooting, unknowingly starting the path to his future.

During elementary school, LeBron began to stand out for his athletic abilities. Not only was he skilled at basketball, but he also excelled in football. His teachers and coaches quickly noticed that he was an exceptional athlete, destined for something special.

In middle school, LeBron started to take basketball more seriously. His impressive height and speed gave him an advantage over other kids his age. He began playing on organized teams, where he continued to improve his skills and dominate the court.

During his freshman year at St. Vincent-St. Mary High School, LeBron joined the varsity basketball team. Despite being one of the youngest players, he played a key role in leading the team to win the state championship, showcasing his potential for greatness.

By his sophomore year, LeBron's incredible talents were gaining attention across the United States. His high school games were covered by sports journalists and even broadcast on television, something extremely rare for a teenage athlete.

At 17 years old, LeBron appeared on the cover of the famous Sports Illustrated magazine, which labeled him as "The Chosen One." The headline cemented his status as the next big star in basketball, and fans everywhere began following his journey.

That same year, LeBron received offers from major college football teams due to his outstanding skills on the field. However, he decided to focus entirely on basketball, his true passion, knowing it was his best path to success.

In 2003, LeBron graduated from high school and declared for the NBA Draft, choosing to skip college and go straight to the pros. His decision was bold, but his talent and confidence left no doubt that he was ready for the next level.

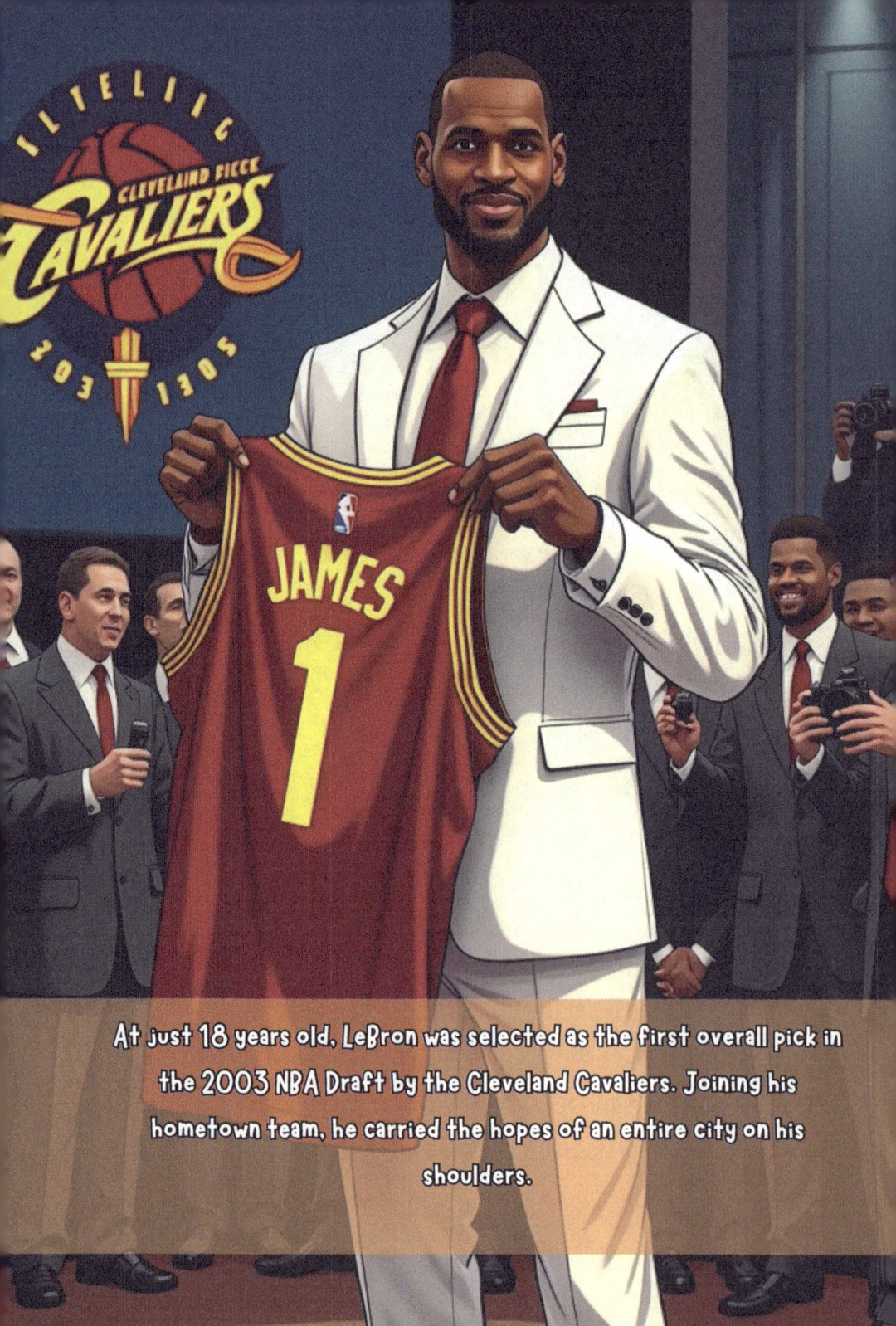

At just 18 years old, LeBron was selected as the first overall pick in the 2003 NBA Draft by the Cleveland Cavaliers. Joining his hometown team, he carried the hopes of an entire city on his shoulders.

On October 29, 2003, LeBron made his NBA debut against the Sacramento Kings. He scored 25 points in his first game, an extraordinary performance for a rookie. The basketball world immediately knew they were witnessing the rise of a future superstar.

During his first NBA season, LeBron James quickly proved he belonged among the best. He won the Rookie of the Year award as the league's top young player, showcasing his incredible skills and potential. It was clear from the start that LeBron was destined for greatness.

In his early years with the Cleveland Cavaliers, LeBron became the team's brightest star. Despite his efforts and jaw-dropping performances, the Cavaliers struggled to win a championship. Still, LeBron's talent and leadership gave fans hope for the future.

In 2007, LeBron led the Cleveland Cavaliers to their first-ever NBA Finals appearance. Though they lost to the experienced San Antonio Spurs, LeBron's determination and skill proved he could compete at the highest level. It was a major milestone in his career.

In 2010, LeBron made the difficult decision to leave the Cavaliers and join the Miami Heat. Teaming up with stars Dwyane Wade and Chris Bosh, he aimed to build a championship-winning team. The move was controversial, but LeBron believed it was necessary for his growth.

LeBron's decision to join the Miami Heat sparked criticism from fans and media alike. He explained that his goal was to win championships and improve as a player. This choice tested his resilience but motivated him to prove his doubters wrong.

In 2012, LeBron achieved his dream of becoming an NBA Champion. Leading the Miami Heat to victory against the Oklahoma City Thunder, he delivered an incredible performance. Winning his first title was a defining moment, proving he was a true champion.

The following year, in 2013, LeBron and the Miami Heat won their second consecutive NBA Championship. This time, they defeated the San Antonio Spurs in an epic seven-game series. LeBron's leadership and dominance on the court were undeniable.

Welcome Back, LEBRON!

In 2014, after four successful seasons in Miami and two NBA titles, LeBron announced his return to the Cleveland Cavaliers. His decision was driven by his desire to bring a championship to his hometown. Fans welcomed him back with open arms.

Returning to Cleveland was personal for LeBron. He wanted to fulfill his promise of winning a championship for the city where he grew up. His determination to succeed for his hometown made this chapter of his career even more meaningful.

In 2016, LeBron delivered on his promise by leading the Cavaliers to a historic NBA Championship. The team defeated the Golden State Warriors in a thrilling seven-game series. It was Cleveland's first NBA title, and LeBron cemented his legacy as a hero.

That 2016 Finals series is remembered for LeBron's iconic performances, including a legendary chase-down block in Game 7. His incredible play shifted the momentum and helped secure the victory. It remains one of the greatest moments in NBA history.

The 2016 championship win was deeply emotional for LeBron. He dedicated the victory to the fans of Cleveland and his family, celebrating the fulfillment of a lifelong dream. The win solidified his place as one of the greatest players ever.

In 2018, LeBron made another big move by signing with the Los Angeles Lakers, one of the most iconic franchises in NBA history. He joined the Lakers to embrace new challenges and continue his pursuit of greatness on and off the court.

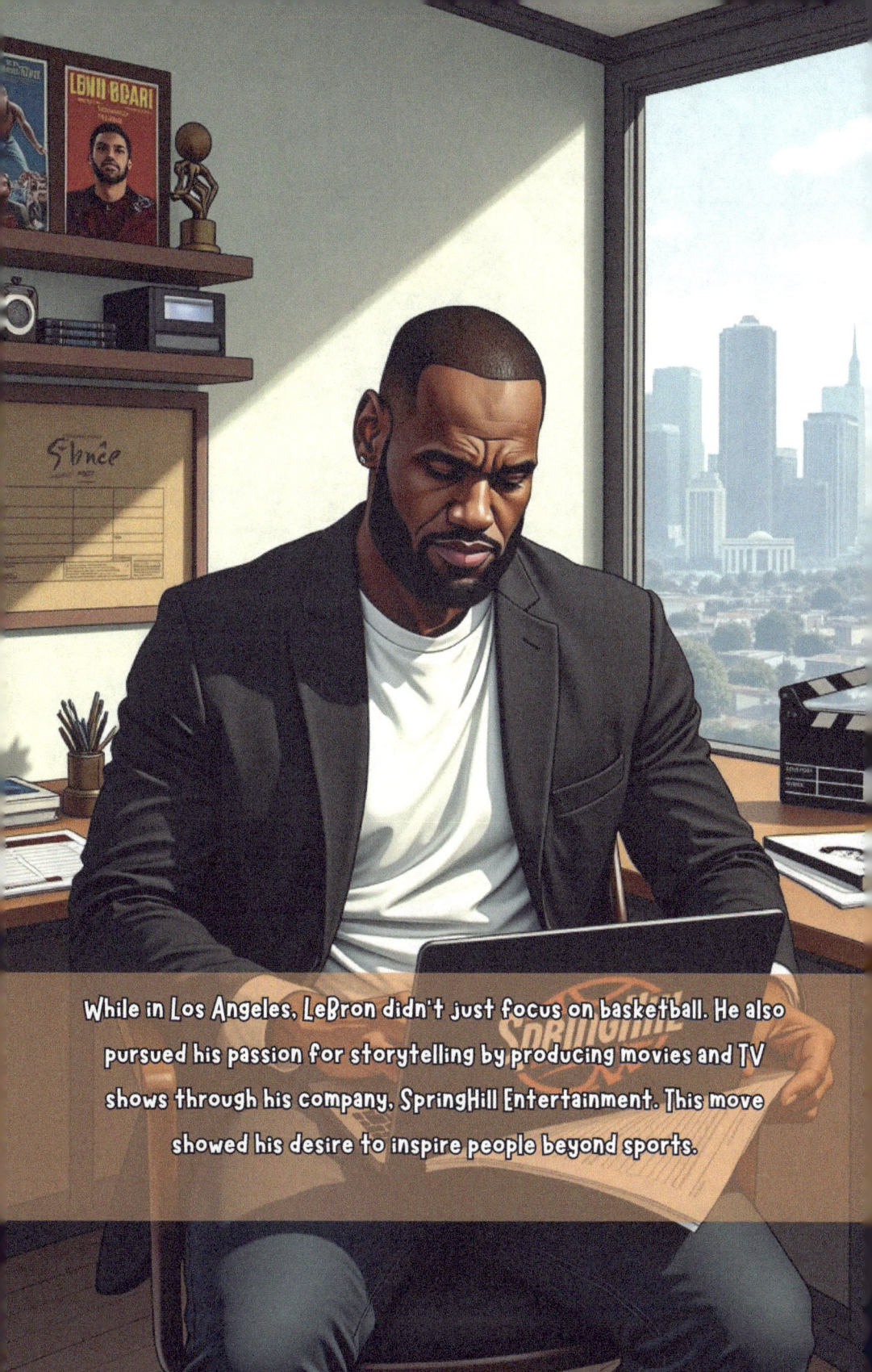

While in Los Angeles, LeBron didn't just focus on basketball. He also pursued his passion for storytelling by producing movies and TV shows through his company, SpringHill Entertainment. This move showed his desire to inspire people beyond sports.

In 2020, LeBron led the Los Angeles Lakers to victory in the NBA Championship, his fourth title overall. The team defeated the Miami Heat in the Finals, and LeBron's leadership and skill were on full display. The win brought pride to Lakers fans around the world.

With this championship, LeBron became one of the few players in NBA history to win titles with three different teams: the Cleveland Cavaliers, Miami Heat, and Los Angeles Lakers. This accomplishment proved his ability to adapt, lead, and succeed anywhere.

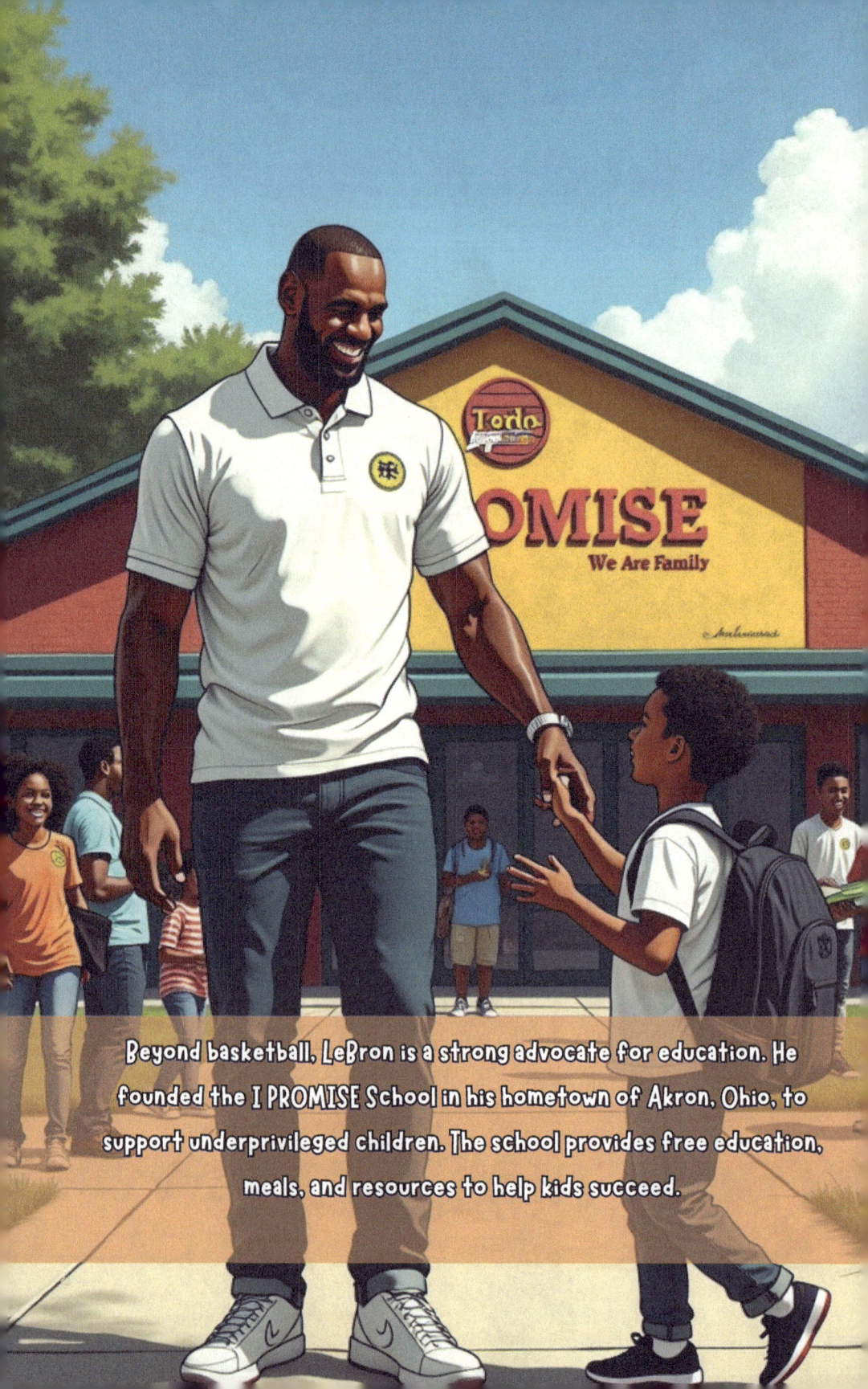

Beyond basketball, LeBron is a strong advocate for education. He founded the I PROMISE School in his hometown of Akron, Ohio, to support underprivileged children. The school provides free education, meals, and resources to help kids succeed.

LeBron has always emphasized the importance of family. He married Savannah, his high school sweetheart, and together they have three children: Bronny, Bryce, and Zhuri. Family remains the driving force behind everything LeBron does.

Off the court, LeBron is a successful businessman with investments in companies like Blaze Pizza and the English soccer team Liverpool FC. His smart financial moves have made him one of the wealthiest and most influential athletes in the world.

LeBron also has a passion for movies. In 2021, he starred in the film "Space Jam: A New Legacy", a sequel to the iconic movie featuring Michael Jordan. The film highlighted his connection to younger generations and love for storytelling.

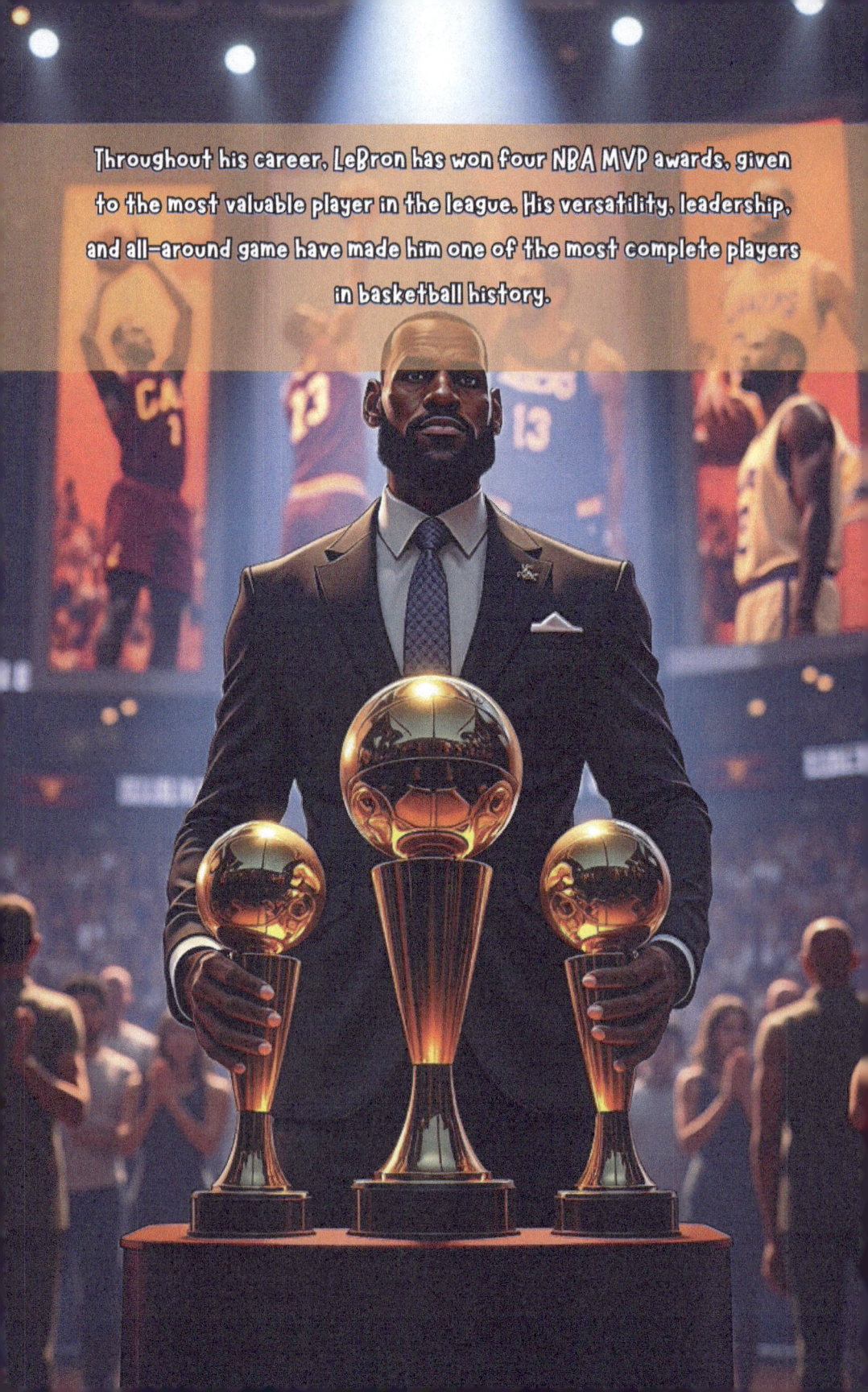

Throughout his career, LeBron has won four NBA MVP awards, given to the most valuable player in the league. His versatility, leadership, and all-around game have made him one of the most complete players in basketball history.

Today, LeBron serves as a role model for young athletes around the world. His motto, "Strive for Greatness", encourages people to dream big, work hard, and believe in themselves. Millions of fans look up to him for inspiration.

Despite winning countless awards and championships, LeBron continues to play with unmatched passion and dedication. He constantly strives to break new records, set higher standards, and show the world that greatness has no limits.

40,000

With over 40,000 career points, LeBron James has made history as one of the NBA's greatest scorers of all time. His consistency, hard work, and talent have set him apart as a true legend of the game.

LeBron James is not only a champion on the court but also a leader off it. He uses his success to inspire others to believe in their dreams, work hard, and never give up. His legacy continues to motivate generations to strive for greatness.

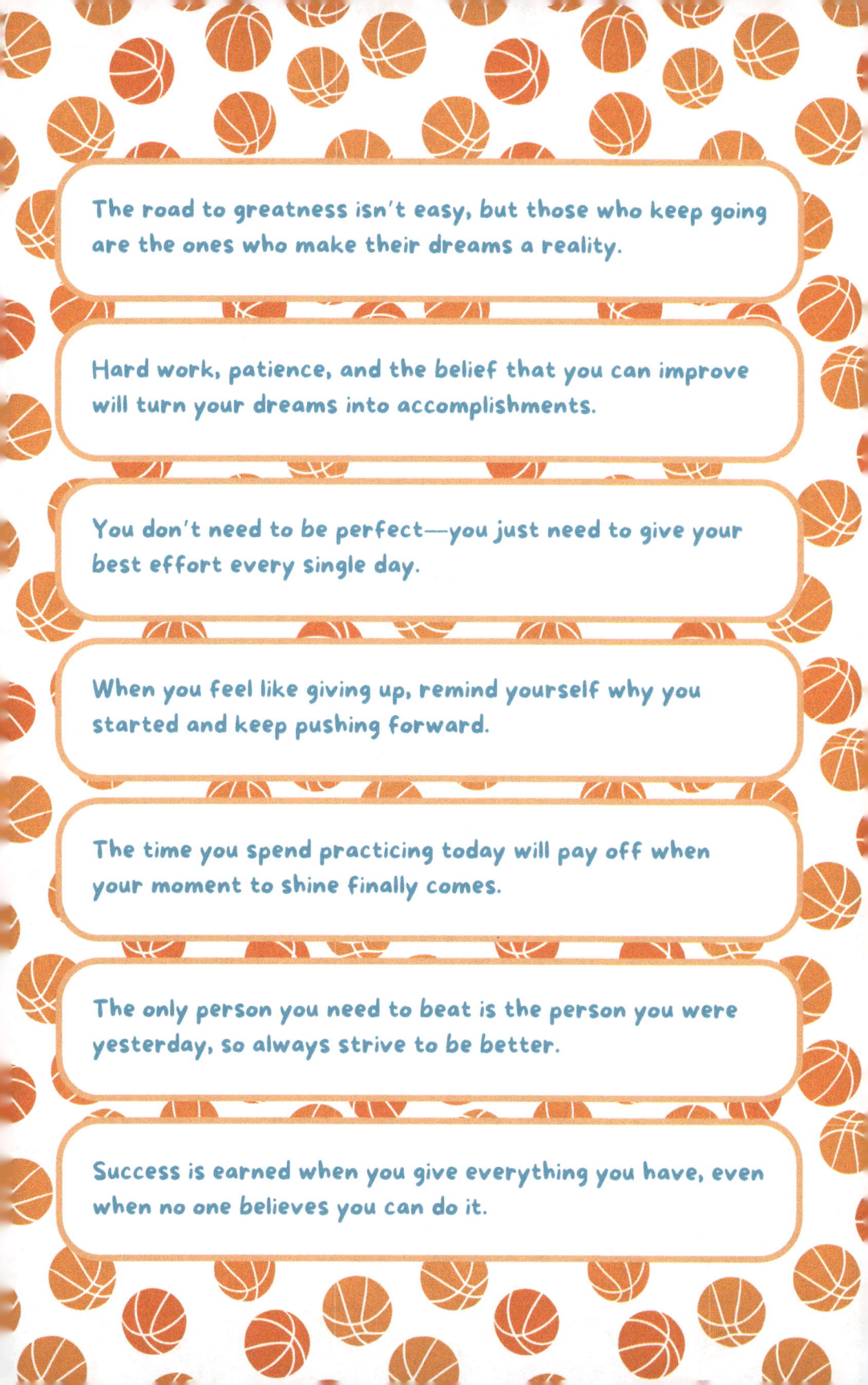

The road to greatness isn't easy, but those who keep going are the ones who make their dreams a reality.

Hard work, patience, and the belief that you can improve will turn your dreams into accomplishments.

You don't need to be perfect—you just need to give your best effort every single day.

When you feel like giving up, remind yourself why you started and keep pushing forward.

The time you spend practicing today will pay off when your moment to shine finally comes.

The only person you need to beat is the person you were yesterday, so always strive to be better.

Success is earned when you give everything you have, even when no one believes you can do it.

Great players are not born—they are made through hard work, focus, and determination every day.

Every practice is an opportunity to grow, improve, and take a step closer to becoming the player you want to be.

Don't compare yourself to others; focus on your progress and trust that your time will come.

Champions are built on discipline, determination, and the will to never quit, no matter how hard it gets.

It doesn't matter how many times you fall—what matters is that you get back up stronger every single time.

Stay focused on your goals and never let anyone tell you that your dreams are impossible.

Every drop of sweat, every tough loss, and every hard-earned win prepares you to be the best version of yourself.

Believe that your dream is possible and work for it like you already know it will come true.

The most successful players are those who learn from their mistakes and turn them into opportunities to improve.

Be proud of how far you've come, but never stop pushing to go even further.

There will be days when it's hard to keep going, but those are the days that will set you apart from the rest.

Greatness isn't about being better than someone else—it's about being the best you can possibly be.

When the game gets tough, remember that your preparation and hard work will carry you through.

Work like you are already the player you dream of becoming, and soon enough, you'll be that player.

Believe in yourself every single day, because confidence is the first step to achieving greatness.

No matter how hard the journey gets, remember that each challenge makes you stronger and more prepared for success.

Every shot you take, every hour you spend practicing, and every mistake you make brings you closer to your dream.

Your dedication in the moments when no one is watching will define who you become when everyone is watching.

Greatness doesn't happen overnight, but every day you work hard, you take one step closer to it.

Never let fear of failure stop you from chasing your dreams—failing is just part of the road to success.

If you believe in your abilities and work harder than everyone else, nothing can stop you from reaching the top.

What are your goals and the milestones you wish to achieve in the future?

1: Did you know LeBron was so good in high school that his games were broadcast on national TV?

LeBron James played for St. Vincent-St. Mary High School in Akron, Ohio, where he became a basketball sensation. His team was so dominant that ESPN began airing their games, something almost unheard of for high school sports at the time. Fans across the country tuned in to watch the young phenom play. He quickly became a household name, even before stepping foot in the NBA. His performances were electrifying, and his games attracted sellout crowds everywhere he went.

2: Did you know he wore the number 6 on the Miami Heat because it was the birth date of his first son?

LeBron switched to the number 6 when he joined the Miami Heat in 2010. This choice wasn't random—it was deeply personal. His son, LeBron James Jr., was born on October 6th, making the number a tribute to his family. During his time in Miami, the number 6 became synonymous with his success, as he led the team to two NBA Championships. It also reflected his respect for Michael Jordan, as he opted not to wear 23 out of admiration.

3: Did you know LeBron is left-handed when writing but shoots a basketball with his right hand?

Although LeBron naturally writes and eats with his left hand, he shoots and dribbles with his right hand. This unique skill set makes him ambidextrous in some ways, giving him a slight edge on the court. He learned to shoot right-handed as a young player, but his left-handed dominance still shows in everyday activities. His ability to use both hands effectively adds versatility to his game, making him a nightmare for defenders.

4: Did you know that as a kid, LeBron also played football and was an excellent wide receiver?

LeBron excelled in football during his middle school and early high school years. Playing as a wide receiver, his height, speed, and athleticism made him nearly unstoppable on the field. Some coaches believed he could have pursued a career in the NFL if he hadn't focused on basketball. His time playing football also helped him develop his incredible hand-eye coordination and toughness, which translated well to his basketball career.

5: Did you know LeBron once thought about quitting basketball to play professional football?

In 2011, during the NBA lockout, LeBron seriously considered trying out for the NFL. Several teams, including the Dallas Cowboys, showed interest in giving him a shot. While he ultimately stuck with basketball, the idea was more than just a dream. LeBron's unique combination of size, strength, and agility would have made him a formidable player in the NFL. This decision shows how multi-talented and versatile he truly is.

6: Did you know LeBron appeared on the cover of Sports Illustrated at just 17 years old?

In 2002, LeBron graced the cover of Sports Illustrated with the headline "The Chosen One." At just 17 years old, he became the youngest athlete to achieve this honor. The cover solidified his status as a future NBA star and put immense pressure on him to succeed. Despite the hype, LeBron embraced the spotlight and exceeded expectations, becoming one of the greatest players in basketball history.

7: Did you know LeBron is a huge fan of the Dallas Cowboys and the New York Yankees?

Growing up, LeBron James was a big fan of sports beyond basketball. He rooted for the Dallas Cowboys in football and the New York Yankees in baseball. Even as his basketball career took off, he remained loyal to these teams. His love for the Yankees was so strong that he sometimes wore a Yankees cap during Cleveland Cavaliers games, which didn't sit well with some local fans. Despite this, his support for these teams shows his lifelong passion for sports in general.

8: Did you know LeBron was the first active NBA player to earn $1 billion during his career?

LeBron James achieved a monumental financial milestone by becoming the first active NBA player to surpass $1 billion in earnings. This figure includes his massive NBA salary, lucrative endorsements, and smart business investments. Companies like Nike, Coca-Cola, and Beats by Dre have contributed to his immense fortune. What makes this even more impressive is that LeBron continues to build his wealth while playing at the highest level, solidifying his status as a global icon on and off the court.

9: Did you know LeBron loves eating cereal for breakfast, especially Fruity Pebbles?

LeBron James has a favorite go-to breakfast: cereal. In particular, he loves Fruity Pebbles. This colorful and sugary cereal has been a favorite of his since childhood. LeBron's love for Fruity Pebbles became so iconic that Nike released a special edition of LeBron sneakers inspired by the cereal's bright colors. It's a fun and relatable detail that shows LeBron still enjoys simple pleasures, just like his fans do.

10: Did you know LeBron starred in the movie "Space Jam: A New Legacy" in 2021?

LeBron James followed in Michael Jordan's footsteps by starring in a Space Jam movie. In 2021, he played himself in "Space Jam: A New Legacy," a sequel to the beloved 1996 film. The movie mixed live action and animation, with LeBron teaming up with Looney Tunes characters like Bugs Bunny. While it received mixed reviews, the film highlighted LeBron's ability to cross over into entertainment, showing he is more than just a basketball player.

11: Did you know LeBron's favorite TV show is "Martin"?

LeBron James has a favorite sitcom from the 1990s: "Martin." The show starred comedian Martin Lawrence and became a classic with its humor and memorable characters. LeBron often talks about how much he enjoyed watching it as a kid and even today. The show's comedic tone and relatable storylines made it a comfort show for LeBron during his free time. It's another example of how he appreciates simple joys in life.

12: Did you know LeBron listens to rap music, especially Jay-Z, before games?

Music plays a big role in LeBron James' pre-game preparation. He often listens to rap music, with Jay-Z being one of his favorite artists. The powerful lyrics and beats help him focus and get into the right mindset before stepping on the court. Jay-Z's music inspires LeBron both as an athlete and as a businessman, as he admires Jay-Z's success. LeBron's connection to music is yet another part of his larger-than-life persona.

13: Did you know LeBron has two dogs named Ghost and Beast?

LeBron James is a big dog lover, and he owns two dogs named Ghost and Beast. The names were inspired by characters from popular TV shows and movies. Ghost, for example, might come from "Game of Thrones," one of LeBron's favorite series. Both dogs are part of the James family, and LeBron often shares pictures of them on social media. They reflect his softer side and show that, even as a superstar, he values his family and pets.

14: Did you know LeBron wears a headband during games because he started balding at a young age?

LeBron James has famously worn a headband during many games throughout his career. While it helps keep sweat out of his eyes, LeBron also admitted that he began balding at a young age. The headband became a part of his signature look, and fans associate it with his on-court dominance. Over time, LeBron embraced his hairline with confidence, showing his fans that being yourself is what matters most.

15: Did you know LeBron gifted $1.3 million to his high school to renovate its basketball gym?

LeBron James never forgot where he came from. To give back to St. Vincent-St. Mary High School, he donated $1.3 million to renovate its basketball gym. The updated gym was named "The LeBron James Arena" in his honor. This gesture not only improved the school's facilities but also inspired young athletes to dream big. It's a perfect example of LeBron's generosity and commitment to helping his community thrive.

16: Did you know LeBron has a tattoo on his back that says "Chosen1"?

When LeBron James was just 17, Sports Illustrated dubbed him the "Chosen One." He embraced this nickname and even got it tattooed across his back. While some might have crumbled under the pressure of such a title, LeBron used it as motivation to succeed. The tattoo is now one of his most recognizable features and serves as a reminder of his journey from a high school phenom to one of the greatest athletes of all time.

17: Did you know LeBron loves playing video games and is a big fan of NBA 2K?

In his downtime, LeBron James loves playing video games. One of his favorites is the NBA 2K series, where he often plays as himself or competes with friends. Gaming is a way for LeBron to unwind and have fun, even during a busy season. He's even been featured on the cover of NBA 2K, solidifying his connection to both basketball and gaming culture. It's yet another way LeBron stays relatable to his younger fans.

18: Did you know LeBron's vertical leap is 40 inches, which allows him to dunk with ease?

LeBron James' incredible athleticism includes a vertical leap of 40 inches, which is far above average for NBA players. This explosive jumping ability allows him to rise above defenders and perform jaw-dropping dunks. His vertical leap is often compared to some of the best jumpers in NBA history. Fans have marveled at his ability to seem as though he's floating in mid-air. Combined with his strength and size, his leaping ability makes him one of the most dominant forces in basketball.

19: Did you know LeBron once played an NBA Finals game with a severely injured hand?

In the 2018 NBA Finals, LeBron James played through a significant hand injury. After an emotional moment earlier in the series, he punched a whiteboard, injuring his hand. Despite the pain, LeBron continued to play at an elite level, scoring, rebounding, and leading his team. His performance under such adversity is a testament to his toughness and dedication to the game. Few fans knew the full extent of his injury until after the series ended, proving how much LeBron sacrifices for his team.

20: Did you know LeBron started the I PROMISE School to help kids from low-income families?

LeBron James believes in giving back, and in 2018, he founded the I PROMISE School in his hometown of Akron, Ohio. This special school focuses on helping at-risk children and their families by providing free education, meals, and support programs. LeBron has said that his own childhood struggles inspired him to create the school. The I PROMISE School represents more than charity—it's LeBron's commitment to changing lives and creating opportunities for the next generation.

21: Did you know LeBron uses a hyperbaric oxygen chamber to recover after games?

LeBron James takes recovery seriously to stay at the top of his game. One of his methods includes using a hyperbaric oxygen chamber, which increases oxygen levels in his body to speed up healing. This advanced recovery technique helps reduce muscle soreness and fatigue after intense games and workouts. It's one of the many ways LeBron invests in his health, ensuring his longevity as a professional athlete. His commitment to recovery is a key reason he's stayed dominant for so long.

22: Did you know LeBron spends over $1 million per year on his body to stay in shape?

LeBron James is known for his incredible work ethic and discipline when it comes to his health. He spends over $1 million annually on trainers, nutritionists, recovery equipment, and workout routines. This includes cryotherapy, massage therapy, and advanced gym facilities. LeBron sees his body as his most valuable asset, and this investment has allowed him to play at an elite level well into his 30s. His dedication sets a new standard for athletes around the world.

23: Did you know LeBron's favorite movie is "Gladiator" starring Russell Crowe?

LeBron James is a big fan of the movie "Gladiator," a historical epic starring Russell Crowe. He admires the film's themes of perseverance, strength, and leadership, which resonate with his own journey. LeBron has often referenced quotes from the movie as inspiration before big games. The story of overcoming challenges and fighting for honor aligns with LeBron's own approach to basketball and life. It's one of his favorite ways to unwind and stay motivated.

24: Did you know LeBron's favorite book is "The Alchemist" by Paulo Coelho?

LeBron James is a big fan of reading, and one of his favorite books is "The Alchemist" by Paulo Coelho. The story is about following one's dreams and finding purpose, themes that resonate deeply with LeBron's own life. He has recommended the book to teammates and fans, saying it helped him reflect on his journey. LeBron's love of reading highlights how he uses books as a way to grow mentally, not just physically. It's a part of his preparation for success both on and off the court.

25: Did you know LeBron doesn't drink coffee because he doesn't like the taste?

Despite his busy lifestyle and demanding schedule, LeBron James avoids coffee. He doesn't like the taste of it and prefers other methods to keep his energy levels up, like water and natural foods. LeBron's approach to nutrition is meticulous, as he avoids junk food and prioritizes a balanced diet to stay in peak shape. His choice to avoid coffee is another example of his discipline and focus on maintaining a healthy lifestyle.

26: Did you know LeBron is afraid of snakes?

Even one of the strongest athletes in the world has fears—and for LeBron James, it's snakes! He has admitted in interviews that he's not a fan of these slithering creatures. Once during a team trip, a prank involving a fake snake scared LeBron so much that he jumped out of his seat. It's a relatable and funny fact that shows even a superstar like LeBron has fears, just like everyone else.

27: Did you know LeBron partnered with Nike to release Fruity Pebbles-themed sneakers?

LeBron's love for Fruity Pebbles cereal became so well known that Nike created a special edition of his signature sneakers inspired by the cereal. The shoes featured bright, colorful designs that mirrored the look of the cereal box. They were an instant hit with fans and sneaker collectors. The partnership reflects how LeBron blends his personal interests with his career, making his brand relatable and fun for his audience.

28: Did you know LeBron played basketball in high school while wearing two pairs of socks?

In high school, LeBron James wore two pairs of socks during basketball games for extra comfort. He believed the added cushioning helped him feel more comfortable while running and jumping. This quirky habit stayed with him for a while, even as he entered the NBA. It's a small detail that highlights LeBron's focus on being his best and finding little ways to improve his game. Many young athletes have adopted this habit, inspired by him.

29: Did you know LeBron is good friends with Dwayne "The Rock" Johnson?

LeBron James and Dwayne "The Rock" Johnson share a close friendship. Both are superstars in their respective fields—basketball and wrestling/acting. The two often support each other's projects and achievements. The Rock has even attended LeBron's games and shared words of encouragement. Their friendship reflects mutual respect and admiration for each other's success and hard work, making them two of the most iconic figures in sports and entertainment.

30: Did you know LeBron has a lifetime contract with Nike, the first of its kind for the brand?

In 2015, LeBron James made history when Nike offered him the first-ever lifetime contract in the company's history. While the exact financial details are private, the deal is believed to be worth over $1 billion. This partnership reflects LeBron's impact not just on basketball but also in the world of sports marketing and branding. Nike saw LeBron's global appeal and his ability to connect with fans of all ages, making him the perfect athlete to represent their brand for life.

31: Did you know LeBron owns part of Liverpool F.C., a famous English soccer team?

LeBron James is not just a basketball star—he's also a savvy businessman. In 2011, he purchased a minority stake in Liverpool F.C., one of the most successful soccer clubs in England. As a co-owner, LeBron has helped promote the team to American fans while also benefiting from its global success. Liverpool's championships and loyal fanbase have made his investment a profitable one. This move highlights LeBron's ability to expand his influence beyond basketball.

32: Did you know LeBron's favorite ice cream flavor is cookies and cream?

When it comes to sweet treats, LeBron James has a favorite: cookies and cream ice cream. Despite his strict diet during the NBA season, LeBron allows himself the occasional indulgence. Cookies and cream is a classic flavor, and LeBron's love for it makes him relatable to fans who enjoy the same treat. Whether he's celebrating a big win or spending time with his family, a bowl of ice cream is one of his simple joys.

33: Did you know LeBron sometimes practices shooting with his eyes closed?

LeBron James uses unique methods to perfect his basketball skills, including practicing shots with his eyes closed. This drill challenges his muscle memory and focus, making his shooting more accurate during games. By training in this way, LeBron can maintain his confidence even under pressure. It's one of the many ways he pushes himself to improve, proving that even the greatest athletes never stop looking for ways to get better.

34: Did you know LeBron loves spaghetti and meatballs and often eats it before games?

Spaghetti and meatballs is one of LeBron James' favorite meals, and he often eats it before games. This classic dish gives him the carbs and energy he needs to perform at his best on the court. While his diet is usually strict, spaghetti and meatballs have remained a staple throughout his career. LeBron's choice shows that comfort food can still play a role in the life of an elite athlete, as long as it's balanced with healthy eating.

35: Did you know LeBron has a tattoo on his chest that says "Family" to honor his loved ones?

LeBron James values family above all else, and he made this clear with a tattoo on his chest that says "Family." This tattoo represents the love and support he's received from his mother, wife, and children throughout his life. Family is a driving force in LeBron's career, and he often speaks about how they inspire him to be the best version of himself. The tattoo serves as a constant reminder of what matters most to him.

36: Did you know LeBron has never competed in the NBA Dunk Contest?

Despite being one of the most spectacular dunkers in NBA history, LeBron James has never participated in the NBA Dunk Contest. Fans have begged him to compete for years, but LeBron has always declined. He has said he prefers to let his in-game dunks speak for themselves. Although he's never competed, his jaw-dropping dunks during games remain unforgettable highlights, proving his ability without the need for a contest.

37: Did you know LeBron owns his own production company called SpringHill Entertainment?

LeBron James is not just an athlete—he's also a successful entrepreneur. He co-founded SpringHill Entertainment, a production company that creates movies, TV shows, and documentaries. Projects like "Space Jam: A New Legacy" and the documentary "More Than a Game" highlight LeBron's vision for storytelling. Through SpringHill, LeBron shares powerful stories that inspire and entertain, proving his influence extends far beyond basketball.

38: Did you know LeBron first played football before focusing on basketball?

Before becoming a basketball superstar, LeBron James was a standout football player in middle school and high school. He played as a wide receiver and was so talented that some believed he could have gone pro in the NFL. His football experience helped him develop skills like speed, coordination, and toughness, which he brought to the basketball court. Ultimately, he chose to focus on basketball, a decision that changed his life forever.

39: Did you know LeBron made a cameo appearance in the movie "Trainwreck" in 2015?

LeBron James showed off his acting skills with a hilarious cameo in the 2015 comedy "Trainwreck," starring Amy Schumer. In the movie, LeBron played himself and showcased his comedic timing, surprising fans with his humor and charm. The role proved that LeBron could shine both on and off the court, leading to more acting opportunities. It's another example of how versatile and talented LeBron truly is.

40: Did you know LeBron enjoys fishing in his free time?

When LeBron James isn't dominating on the court, he enjoys spending time outdoors, especially fishing. Fishing allows LeBron to relax and unwind, providing a peaceful break from his busy schedule. He often shares photos of his fishing trips with friends and family on social media. It's a hobby that helps him recharge mentally and emotionally, showing the importance of balance in his life.

41: Did you know LeBron has invested in Blaze Pizza, a popular pizza chain?

LeBron James is not only a basketball star but also a smart investor. He invested in Blaze Pizza, a fast-casual pizza chain that became incredibly successful. LeBron's involvement helped the brand grow rapidly, as fans flocked to try the pizza endorsed by their favorite athlete. His investment in Blaze Pizza shows his business savvy and ability to identify great opportunities outside of basketball.

42: Did you know LeBron loves animated movies like "Finding Nemo" and "The Lion King"?

LeBron James has a soft spot for animated movies, with "Finding Nemo" and "The Lion King" being among his favorites. These classic films remind him of his childhood and the lessons they teach about family, courage, and perseverance. LeBron often watches them with his kids, sharing moments of laughter and joy. It's a fun fact that makes him even more relatable to fans who love the same movies.

43: Did you know LeBron taught himself to do a backflip in middle school?

LeBron James showed off his athleticism even as a kid when he taught himself how to do a backflip. In middle school, he practiced until he could land the move perfectly. This impressive skill amazed his friends and showed his natural ability to control his body. While he doesn't perform backflips anymore, it's a fun fact that highlights just how talented and determined LeBron was, even at a young age.

44: Did you know LeBron reads books to calm his mind before big games?

LeBron James has a unique way of preparing for games—he reads books to relax and focus. Whether it's fiction, self-help, or biographies, reading helps him clear his mind and get into the right mental space. LeBron believes that staying mentally sharp is just as important as being physically ready. His love of reading sets a great example for young athletes, showing the value of lifelong learning and balance.

45: Did you know LeBron texts motivational quotes to his teammates at 3 a.m.?

LeBron James is known for his leadership, and one way he inspires his teammates is by sending motivational texts. Sometimes, these messages arrive as early as 3 a.m. LeBron believes in staying focused and positive, even when others are sleeping. His dedication to motivating his team shows his passion for winning and his role as a leader on and off the court. It's this drive that makes him a great teammate and role model.

46: Did you know LeBron has a collection of over 400 pairs of sneakers?

LeBron James is a huge sneakerhead, and his collection boasts over 400 pairs of sneakers. Many of these shoes are special editions or custom designs made just for him. As a Nike athlete, LeBron has released his own signature line of sneakers, which have become extremely popular among fans. His love for shoes started when he was a kid, and now his collection reflects both his passion for style and his legendary career.

47: Did you know LeBron wore the number 23 because of his idol, Michael Jordan?

LeBron James chose to wear the number 23 in honor of his basketball idol, Michael Jordan. Jordan was a role model for LeBron growing up, inspiring him to dream big and work hard. LeBron wanted to carry on the legacy of greatness that the number 23 represented. Although he later switched to number 6 during his time with the Miami Heat, the number 23 remains a special symbol of LeBron's admiration for one of the greatest players in NBA history.

48: Did you know LeBron uses cryotherapy chambers to speed up muscle recovery?

LeBron James uses cryotherapy, a recovery method that involves exposing the body to extremely cold temperatures for short periods. This helps reduce inflammation, relieve soreness, and accelerate muscle healing after tough games and workouts. Cryotherapy is just one of the many advanced techniques LeBron uses to stay in top shape. His commitment to recovery has allowed him to maintain peak performance throughout his long and successful career.

49: Did you know LeBron owns a custom jeweled basketball worth over $20,000?

LeBron James has a one-of-a-kind basketball made entirely of jewels and valued at over $20,000. This unique piece of art was a gift and symbolizes LeBron's success and influence in the world of basketball. While it's not something he plays with, the jeweled basketball is a fun and luxurious part of his collection. It's a reminder of how far he's come from his humble beginnings in Akron, Ohio.

50: Did you know LeBron designed a children's book series about overcoming challenges?

LeBron James helped create a children's book series that encourages kids to dream big and overcome challenges. The books share positive messages about hard work, determination, and teamwork—values that LeBron lives by. He hopes these stories will inspire young readers to believe in themselves and strive for greatness. Through this project, LeBron continues to make an impact off the court, showing his commitment to empowering the next generation.

51: Did you know LeBron has performed onstage with Drake at concerts?

LeBron James has a close friendship with rapper Drake, and the two have shared the stage at several concerts. LeBron has been seen hyping up the crowd and enjoying the music alongside Drake. Their bond highlights LeBron's love for music and his ability to connect with other artists. Moments like these show that LeBron is not only a superstar on the court but also someone who knows how to have fun and entertain.

52: Did you know LeBron loves to cook breakfast for his family on Sundays?

Despite his busy schedule, LeBron James enjoys spending quality time with his family, and one of his favorite traditions is cooking breakfast on Sundays. He often prepares pancakes, eggs, and other family favorites. LeBron says these moments allow him to relax and bond with his loved ones. It's a glimpse into his personal life and shows that, despite his fame, he's a dedicated family man who values simple joys.

53: Did you know LeBron can solve a Rubik's Cube in under a minute?

LeBron James has a hidden talent: he can solve a Rubik's Cube in less than a minute. He uses this skill as a mental exercise to challenge himself and improve his focus. Solving the cube requires patience, strategy, and quick thinking—qualities that LeBron applies on the basketball court as well. Fans are often amazed by his ability to master such a tricky puzzle, proving that he excels both physically and mentally.

54: Did you know LeBron collects luxury watches, including Rolex and Audemars Piguet?

LeBron James is a fan of luxury watches and has an impressive collection featuring brands like Rolex and Audemars Piguet. Each watch is a symbol of his success and hard work, and he often wears them during important events and public appearances. For LeBron, these timepieces are more than just accessories—they represent the milestones he's achieved throughout his career. His love for watches reflects his appreciation for quality and craftsmanship.

Thank you for purchasing this book!

If you enjoyed it, subscribe to our newsletter at VendittoEditore.com or scan the QR code below to receive free updates, including coloring pages, quizzes, and many more fun facts about Lebron James

Made in the USA
Las Vegas, NV
01 April 2025